sharon p[...]

STRESSED?
How to handle the pressure

First published 2009
Copyright © 2009

British Library Cataloguing in Publication Data.
A catalogue record for this book is available from the British Library.

ISBN 978-1-906381-54-7

Published by Autumn House, Grantham, Lincolnshire.
Printed in Thailand.

UPFRONT

Some degree of stress is good for us, but when it builds up we need to learn how to deal with it effectively as the results can be damaging.

In this book we look at the causes of stress, its health impact, foods which help to alleviate or aggravate stress, environmental triggers, and suggestions for combating stress and living a more balanced lifestyle. We also explore the spiritual renewal we find in Christ as we are reminded in 1 Peter 5:7: 'Casting all your care upon him; for he cares for you.' (*New King James Version*.)

When facing a highly pressured situation, the body produces higher levels of hormones like cortisol and adrenaline, which, among other symptoms, cause changes such as the constriction and dilation of arteries, and increased breathing and heart-rate.

The causes of stress are highly individual, but can be placed into three broad categories of stressors, namely, pressures, frustrations and conflicts. If these stressors involve central aspects of your life or persist for extended periods of time, they are more likely to result in severe distress and disruption of daily functioning with resulting negative physical and emotional impact.

An article in *USA Today* entitled 'A Mess of Stress' carried the results of a survey identifying the major sources of stress for typical Americans. The research was conducted on 501 adults by Research and Forecast Icl., and yielded the following results:

36% stated that work was the biggest source of stress in their lives
22% cited money
10% said children
7% said health

5% stated marriage
5% cited parents
19% asserted that they had little stress in their daily life
Only 5% said that they had no stress at all.

To assess your level of stress, try Dr Rahe's Life Changes Stress Test (via Google). It will be most revealing!

SIGNS AND SYMPTOMS

How does stress manifest itself? In a 'normal' stress response, the physical effects of stress could be lifesaving. This is the 'fight or flight' response when experiencing fear or threat, where our body releases a rush of adrenaline, giving us the impetus we need to fight the threat or fear or to run away. This is the body's emergency response. Changes occur in the cardiovascular and metabolic system, increasing pulse, blood pressure and sugar levels and blood is diverted to vital organs such as the lungs, heart and muscles.

When suffering ongoing stress, the body instigates the 'fight or flight' response continuously, and we experience a variety of symptoms which generally fall into four categories:

- **physical** – our body's response

- **behavioural** – the things we do

- **emotional** – what we feel

- **psychological** – our individual thinking style

Physical symptoms

Aches and pains, breathlessness, change in menstrual cycle, chest pain and/or palpitations, constipation, diarrhoea, headaches, indigestion, muscle twitches, nausea, recurrence of previous illnesses/allergies, skin conditions, sleep problems, tiredness, tightness in chest, weight loss or weight gain.

Behavioural symptoms

Accident-prone, change in sleeping patterns, declining work performance, drinkers and smokers increase habit, inability to relax, inability to express feelings, loss of appetite, loss of libido, overeating, over-reacting to issues, poor time management, poor judgement, withdrawing from family and friends.

Emotional symptoms/feelings

Anger, anxiety, decrease in confidence/self-esteem, feeling helpless, feelings of guilt, feelings of shame, feeling out of control, increasingly cynical, lack of enthusiasm, mood swings, poor concentration, tension.

Psychological symptoms/recurrent negative thoughts and expressions

'I can't cope,' 'I don't know what to do,' 'I don't seem to be able to get on top of things,' 'I keep forgetting where I put things,' 'I'm a failure,' 'I should be able to cope,' loss of judgement, 'Nobody understands,' 'What's the point?' 'Why is everyone getting at me?'

Recognising what stresses us and being aware of the symptoms will enable us to take action to reduce the negative effects.

ARE YOU AT RISK?

Everyone has a different threshold at which they become stressed. It has nothing to do with weakness, as stress can affect anyone. Professor Stephen Palmer from the Centre for Stress Management in London explains stress as 'an interaction between the person and the environment.' He further states: 'Stress is about too many demands and a lack of control. But it also depends on how the person perceives the situation.'

Individual response to stress varies greatly and is dependent on a number of factors, namely:

- genetic makeup
- personality type and temperament
- constitutional strengths and weaknesses
- general health and well-being
- life change events
- environmental stressors.

Is stress on the increase, and who is most affected?

In September 2000, Channel 4 commissioned a survey on stress. The poll was conducted by Taylor Nelson Sofres Phonebus, who interviewed 534 adults aged 16 and over, in full and part-time work.

The survey revealed some fascinating facts about our stressful lives:

- The most stressed-out region in the survey was the south-east, with 49% reporting an increase in stress but relating it to work issues.

- People living in the south-west found their stress levels most unacceptable. This amounted to 27% compared with 15% nationwide.

- The highest percentage suffering from increased stress were widowed, divorced or separated. Sixty-two percent in this group said stress had escalated.

- Forty-one percent of people working full or part-time said their stress levels had increased in the previous twelve months. This suggests 11.5 million British workers feeling stress levels rise in that time. However, part-time workers were less likely to report increased stress levels, with 29% saying they felt more stress, compared with 45% of full-timers.

- Forty-three percent of workers with children reported increased stress compared with 40% without children.

- Forty-two percent of men said their stress levels had risen compared with 40% of women.

- People who were married were slightly less likely than average (at 40%) to report stress levels going up.

- Younger people were more likely to say stress levels had gone up. Forty-six percent of 16 to 24-year-olds said stress had risen. Among 25 to 34-year-olds, the figure fell to 41%, increasing slightly to 42% of 35 to 44-year-olds, and reducing to 38% of 45 to 54-year-olds, and 36% of 55 to 64-year-olds.

RISK FACTORS AND PRACTICAL TIPS TO COMBAT STRESS

Staley, a facilitator who runs the CALM programme which aims to alleviate stress, says: 'Much of our lives are subject to "rainbow chasing", we go to bed, but not to sleep; eat food but not to satisfy our appetites; take medicine but do not improve our health; live in beautiful houses which are not happy homes; and buy luxuries which do not bring us contentment.' He further states: 'Most people are now prey to the tensions of living in one place, working in another and taking leisure in a third.'

We need to find ways to deal with stress before it deals with us!

Quick tips

1. Trust God to take over – he's in charge anyway.

2. Some stress is necessary to motivate or inspire productivity.

3. Too much stress (pressure that continues for too long and leaves you feeling out-of-control) can be harmful.

4. Recognise symptoms early.

5. Identify cause.

6. Seek practical solutions like the following:

a) Write down in order of priority what stresses you.

b) Talk to a friend or counsellor – unloading helps.

c) Accept what cannot be changed – it brings some relief.

d) Try to avoid too many life change events in the course of a twelve-month period.

7. Let go of resentment – it's toxic to the mind and induces stress.

8. Take time for rest and relaxation – it rejuvenates.

9. Avoid junk food – it can aggravate stress symptoms.

10. Maintain regular exercise to burn excess adrenaline.

A popular check for identifying stress was devised by two American psychologists, Holmes and Rahe*, who created a scale of forty-three life events considered to be stressful. Each event is scored according to the degree of stress associated with the activity. According to the scale, the top ten most stressful life events are:

1. death of a partner
2. divorce
3. separation from partner
4. imprisonment
5. death of a close family member

6. personal illness
   or injury

7. marriage

8. dismissal from
   work

9. change of job

10. retirement.

*(Holmes and Rahe, 1967, 'The social readjustment rating scale', *Psychosomatic Medicine*, 11: 213-18.)

Are you feeling stressed? Take time to reflect on the cause, but realise that there is always a way of dealing with it. Helen Keller has this advice: 'Although the world is full of suffering it is also full of the overcoming of it.'

STRESS AND WORK

Is your job stressing you?

This section comes with a disclaimer: **If your job features as highly stressed in the following list the writer cannot be held responsible for any stress this discovery may cause you.**

Modern life in the Western World today consists of longer working hours and associated escalating stress levels.

Europeans under stress

The European Foundation for the Improvement of Living and Working Conditions in 2001 found that most Europeans are working in stressful conditions. It reports Dr Lennart Levi, Professor of Psychosocial Medicine at the Karolinksa Institute, Sweden, stating that more than a quarter (28%) of the European workforce complains of stress.

Further studies by The Public & Commercial Services Union undertaking research in 2003 produced the following alarming statistics:

- UK employees work the longest hours in Europe

- Forty-two percent regularly work more than 48 hours a week

- Sixty percent of all work absences in the UK are caused by stress

- Stress costs the UK economy £8billion a year

- Fifty-two percent of employees often find work means they are too tired to enjoy their free time

- One in three UK residents find their working hours prevent them spending enough time with their family

How stressful is *your* job?

Britain's 20 most stressful jobs*

1. Prison officer
2. Police
3. Social work
4. Teaching
5. Ambulance service
6. Nursing
7. Medicine
8. Fire-fighting
9. Dentistry
10. Mining

11. Armed forces
12. Construction
13. Management
14. Acting
15. Journalism
16. Linguist
17. Film producer
18. Professional sport
19. Catering/hotel industry
20. Public transport

* Research by Professor Cary Cooper from University of Manchester's Institute of Science and Technology in 1997, assessing 104 jobs.

Over 60% of the 104 jobs showed increases in stress levels from 1985 to 1997.

If *you* are experiencing work-related stress, then you need to raise your concerns with your employer.

Current law encourages employers to have workplace policies which reflect flexible working practices. This gives employees a chance of a good work-life balance by allowing them more say in how they undertake their working life. When this is achieved, research found that employees are more productive and live healthier lives.

STRESS AND WORK –
Health impact

Stress is causing physical ill health, emotional distress and other problems for many working people. The latest survey by the International Stress Management Association found more than half (53%) of working people reported suffering from stress in the past twelve months. The study, released on National Stress Awareness Day in 2001, found one in four people had taken time off sick due to stress in the previous year.

Workers who reported being very stressed had a range of health and behaviour problems, from poor mental health and back pain to excessive drinking and smoking.

In 2000 'The Scale of Occupational Stress: The Bristol stress and health at work study' discovered clear links between high stress scores and adverse working conditions, such as having too much to do and not being supported by managers.

The survey enquired which symptoms people had suffered in the last twelve months due to workplace stress. The results identified:

- irritability (29%)

- changes in sleep patterns (29%)

- inability to relax (28%)

- changes in eating patterns (18%)
- inability to concentrate (17%)
- anxiety or depression (16%)
- physical illness (8%)
- memory loss (8%)
- substance misuse, such as drugs/drinking or increased smoking (5%).

The Chartered Management Institute and PPP healthcare undertook a survey in 2000 which found a quarter of executives had taken sick leave in the past year as a result of stress. Almost three-quarters of executives claimed workplace stress was damaging their health, happiness and home life, as well as their performance at work.

Having control over one's job appears to enhance one's ability to cope with stress.

One way of assessing whether you are coping well with stress is to ascertain where you fit on the 'burnout scale'. This highlights stress 'warning signs' on a scale ascending from stage one to stage four.

Stage one: involves bringing work home, spending too little time with family or friends, and having doubts about coping.

Stage two: includes tiredness and anxiety, working long hours and becoming irritable.

Stage three: escalates to increased anger and resentment, extreme exhaustion and lack of enjoyment in life.

Stage four: denotes full scale withdrawal, illness, absenteeism, extreme distress and alcohol or drug abuse or other addictive behaviour.

It is possible to manage pressures by facing them in a different way.

THE FOOD FACTOR

When we are stressed our bodies produce stress hormones, which release fatty acids and sugars to help us cope. Food choices can impact our stress response.

Experts in the field of stress management have identified the following key foods which aggravate stress reactions in certain people.

Avoid:

- high intake of refined sugars such as chocolate, cake, biscuits and sugar-based foods.

- foods with a high-fat content.

- stimulants such as coffee or cola-based drinks.

Sugar

Refined sugar produces quick energy surges, giving a short-term high. The body has to produce extra insulin to deal with the influx of sugar and this causes a drop in blood sugar levels, resulting in your feeling more tired and yearning for more sweet snacks. A self-defeating cycle occurs.

Vitamins and minerals

Insufficient magnesium, zinc and vitamin B6 (found in vegetables, fruit and pulses) has been linked to depression. However, too much of some nutrients can over-stimulate the nervous system, leading to feelings of anxiety.

Stimulants

- Alcohol dehydrates, acts as a depressant and can increase mood swings, depressive symptoms and aggression.

- Avoid coffee, tea, cola drinks and chocolate, as these contain varying amounts of caffeine which acts as a stimulant.

The adrenal gland may become overactive due to stress. The use of stimulants can encourage the adrenal system to work harder than necessary.

Saturated fats

Avoid saturated fats. A high-fat diet can lead to raised levels of cholesterol which are linked to coronary heart disease and high blood pressure. Since stress is also believed to contribute to heart problems and raised blood pressure, extra care should be taken to avoid diet risks.

Junk food

Try to avoid 'fast foods' as they usually contain unhealthy levels of fat, salt and additives.

Salt

Avoid excessive amounts of salt (sodium) which can also raise blood pressure, leading to possible heart problems. About a quarter of the salt we need is found naturally in food. However, many processed foods contain unhealthily high salt levels.

Water

Drinking adequate water helps flush out toxins (enhancing well-being) and keeps the kidneys working well. Current medical advice suggests up to two litres daily. Avoid sugary flavourings, as this encourages the body to produce more insulin.

Some people overeat when they feel stressed, while others lose their appetite.

Dietary balance

Research shows that we can make nutrition and lifestyle choices that decrease vulnerability to stress, increase the ability to cope when stress occurs, and protect against negative outcomes of stress.

Maintaining a healthy balanced diet is important, as chronic stress can affect the body's nutritional needs, metabolism, brain function, mood, immunity and general health, increasing the risk of certain diseases and affecting longevity.

The body utilises energy at a faster rate when stressed. This change has an impact on metabolism and, consequently, the requirements of nutrients.

- Stress hormones accelerate heart-rate; increase muscle tension; elevate blood pressure, cholesterol and triglyceride levels which increase the metabolic rate.

- Increased metabolism can stimulate an increase in the use and excretion of carbohydrates, fats, proteins and nutrients such as vitamins A, B complex, C, D, E and K, and minerals such as calcium, chromium, magnesium, phosphorous, potassium, selenium and zinc.

Nutrition choices can have a profound effect on the stress response:

- Vulnerability to stress increases with poor diet and can impair brain function.

- Skipping meals drops blood sugar levels, causing reactions in the nervous system, which can create feelings of anxiety.

- Depressed individuals may crave sugary and/or fatty foods during stress.

- Excess amounts of sugars and refined foods can diminish thiamine, niacin, B12, magnesium and calcium. Reduced levels of these nutrients can increase nervousness, anxiety, fatigue, irritability and nervous system response, leading to increased stress sensitivity and tendency to aggression.

- Caffeine increases stress hormones, irritability, dehydration, and encourages loss of calcium, magnesium and B vitamins.

- Excess protein (particularly animal) creates metabolic stress and robs the bones of calcium.

A stress-buster diet could consist of the following:

- **Omega 3 fats** have been suggested by research to have a calming and anti-depressive effect on the nervous system, enhancing brain health and mental well-being. Rich sources are flax seeds, walnuts and almonds.

- **High-fibre diet,** rich in fresh fruits, vegetables, nuts and whole grains, maintains appetite satisfaction, discouraging snacking, and provides vitamins A, C, B6 and B vitamins niacin, thiamine, riboflavin and folate for good nervous-system health. High-fibre diets improve mood and curb afternoon drowsiness.

- **Minerals** such as magnesium, iron, selenium, zinc, phosphorus and calcium are provided by the above foods and provide significant stress protection, enhance energy and alertness, and encourage good nerve impulse transmission.

Eat well!

GENDER DIFFERENCES

Studies show equal numbers of men and women complaining of stress. However, they are stressed by different things and also react in different ways.

Stressors for women

Poor work-life balance – Many working women carry the lion's share of childcare, housework and caring for older relatives.

Pregnancy –
Brings hormonal changes,
pregnancy related symptoms,
altered body image.

New baby –
can involve lone parenting,
relationship difficulties with
partner, financial concerns,
career break or change,
postnatal depression.

Children –
bring high dependency. A parenting magazine survey found that 51% of full-time mothers felt regularly stressed, compared to 29% of working women without children.

Caring for relatives –
brings repetitive and demanding chores. There are 6.8 million carers (mostly women) in Britain looking after disabled or frail elderly relatives.

Bereavement –
Women are more likely to
suffer bereavement as they
generally live longer than men.

Stressors for men

Peter Baker, editor of the website *malehealth.co.uk,* states, 'Stress is not just about having a hyperactive lifestyle.' He adds: 'Having no role and being hard-up is very stressful too.'

Unemployment –
loss of self-esteem, financial
difficulties.

Work changes –
outsourcing, longer hours,
temporary contracts.

Changing roles –
not the main breadwinner.

Modern man –
Society now expects men to
devote more time to home
and family as well as work.
Subsequently, after working long
hours men feel pressured to
be domesticated, entertain the
children and be ideal partners.

How women cope

Women are generally better than men at seeking help when stressed, and are more comfortable sharing their feelings and talking about everyday life challenges. Twice as many women as men see their doctors about anxiety, depression and stress, rather than waiting for a physical problem to develop. Carole Spiers, an occupational stress counsellor, agrees that women often cope with several demands because they are naturally more 'multi-tasked'.

How men cope

Men are less likely than women to talk about how they feel and seek help from a doctor or anyone else. Most men wait until medical symptoms of stress emerge, such as chest pains, headaches and stomach problems, before visiting their GP. They tend to choose escape routes like exercise, drinking, smoking, or driving aggressively.

The mental-health charity Mind
reports that three-quarters of
suicides in the UK are by men.
Research suggests men suffer
from depression just as frequently
as women, but are less likely
to be diagnosed by a doctor.

Reports indicate that both men
and women benefit equally from
effective stress management.

IMPACT ON YOUTH
Student stress

According to the Student Living
Report 2002, more than half of
students (53%) said they had
become more stressed since
starting university.

Some of the main reasons blamed for student stress are:

- financial worries
- debt
- exam pressure
- burden of coursework
- relationship problems
- juggling university work with other commitments.

The report found one in four students experienced severe financial difficulty. The survey revealed students beginning the academic year in September 2001 with an average £4,203 debt. To make ends meet, nearly half (43%) worked part-time during term-time and 59% of those who worked believed it interfered with their studies.

Financial hardship meant that most students relied on their families for extra support. A total of 87% of students received some financial help from their parents, guardian, partner or other family member. Nearly half (44%) said this caused friction.

The 1999 NUS Student Hardship Survey found that after paying for accommodation students living away from home outside London were left with just £23.30 a week to cover bills, food, clothes, books and travel.

Ann Heyno, media spokesperson for the Heads of University Counselling Services, says: 'There is an awful lot of pressure on students these days to succeed . . . especially because they have invested a lot of money in their education and so they feel they have to do incredibly well.'

Heyno also reports the following stressors:

- Parental expectation
- Bereavement at home
- Parental break-up
- University far from home
- Inadequate parental support.

Latest figures show that from 1983 to 1994, student suicides rose from 2.4 to 9.7 per 100,000.

Youth stress clinics have become popular in recognition of the stress impact on young people. These clinics address issues relating to anger, low self-esteem and depression brought on by stressful life events. The Youth Stress Centre in Glasgow tackles the following:

- emotions, feelings, and stress

- dealing with anger and conflict

- self-awareness

- health and well-being
- understanding relationships
- assertiveness
- peer support
- exam stress
- coping skills

Methods include

- one-to-one counselling
- discussion
- group work and games
- breathing and relaxation exercises
- role-play and expressive arts.

The results?
An impressive

- **94%** improved relationships
- **97%** increased confidence and self-esteem
- **94%** improved personal skills.

Stress management improves mental well-being!

THE COST OF CARING

One in eight adults – almost six million people in Britain – is a carer. According to the 1995 General Household Survey published in 1998, while the average age is between 45 and 64, up to 50,000 carers are believed to be under 18. Although most carers are women, about 42% are men.

What carers do

Carers look after people who due to frailty, illness or disability are unable to look after themselves. Care can include tending individuals through physical, mental or terminal illnesses like cancer or AIDS. Nearly half of all carers juggle their role with paid work.

Stress impact

Although the nature and extent of caring varies among carers, stress is an experience common to most. A study by Carers UK, published in 2004, entitled 'In Poor Health: The Impact of Caring On Health', found that carers providing high levels of care were twice as likely as non-carers to suffer ill health.

Another Carers UK study, 'Ignored and Invisible?' found more than half of UK carers have been treated for a stress-related illness since becoming a carer. Additionally it was found that if they don't get a break, carers are twice as likely to suffer from mental health problems. The report, 'Stress in Informal Carers of Hospitalised Elderly Patients', published in 1995, found that 47% of carers suffered depression.

Causes of stress

- Juggling work and caring
- Financial difficulties if having to give up paid work
- On call twenty-four hours a day or caring long hours
- Other family members feel neglected
- Strain on personal relationships
- Inability to take a holiday or arrange short breaks
- Neglect of self and own needs.

Support for carers

A range of support services for carers may help prevent and manage stress. These include:

- **information** – on services, support groups, benefits and so on

- **advice and advocacy** – to access and negotiate with local services

- **time off** – for holidays, day trips or just a break from routine

- **meeting others** – talking to other carers can be a lifeline

- **therapies** – stress relief interventions, like massage, aid relaxation and provide a break

- **stress management** – empowers individuals to find ways to deal effectively with their stress.

The key components of the Carers and Disabled Children Act 2000 gives carers the right to an assessment, offers direct payments to carers and short-term break vouchers.

IMPACT ON AGEING

The hormone cortisol

Increased levels of this hormone are associated with abnormal ageing processes. We need to identify simple steps we can take in order to gain control of our life, reduce our stress level and live a longer and healthier life.

Effects of cortisol

When we become stressed, it leads to the increased accumulation of the hormone cortisol. This vital hormone is often referred to as the 'stress hormone' as it is activated in the stress response. It increases blood pressure, blood sugar levels and has an immuno-suppressive action, which means that the efficacy of the immune system is reduced.

Cortisol regulates cardiovascular function and affects blood pressure. It enables the body's use of fatty acids as a source of energy for our muscles and impacts our body's use of proteins, fats and carbohydrates.

Dangers of excess cortisol

While cortisol may be an essential hormone in maintaining good health, excess cortisol may lead to adverse health conditions. A prolonged increase in cortisol leads to a decrease in brain cells, a reduction of bone density and a loss of vital muscle mass. Current research suggests that excess cortisol, brought on by excess stress, will reduce our longevity.

Research from the University of California indicated the impact of stress on the cell. They found that chromosomes age ten years with psychological stress.

Advice

- If you control your stress, you can control your cortisol.

Applying these simple techniques will help to lower stress:

- Maintain a consistent and healthy diet.

- Avoid caffeine – it aggravates the stress response.

- Don't use alcohol.

- Establish a routine bedtime and get adequate sleep every night.

- Moderate physical exercise helps reduce stress.

- Say 'no'.

- Prioritise your 'to-do' list.

- Improve time management – over-scheduling is a primary cause of stress.

- Set realistic goals.

- Increase your prayer life.

- Talk to someone you trust about how you are feeling.

- Get a massage.

Key points:

- We release cortisol in response to stressors placed on our body.

- We can lower cortisol by reducing stress.

- If you reduce your stress, you lengthen your life.

THOUGHT PATTERNS

Research has demonstrated that the way we think has a direct relationship with how we feel and behave. It is clear that our thinking style affects how stressed we get in any given situation. This, in turn, has an effect on general well-being and health.

Additionally, negative thoughts can lead to negative outcomes, as negative thinking accentuates the challenges we face. This, in turn, can escalate a situation, making it more of a drama and crisis than it is in reality. As a result, we experience more stress.

The American Psychological Association's *Journal of Personality and Social Psychology* published research in 2002 on the effects of thought patterns on stress. It revealed that optimists tend to have happier lives and are generally healthier, regardless of the degree of stress they experience.

A study by Researchers at the Harvard School of Public Health and the Department of Veterans' Affairs in Boston discovered that people who viewed the world more optimistically had half the risk of coronary heart disease compared to their more pessimistic counterparts.

Another study by staff at Brigham and Women's Hospital and the Harvard Medical School suggests that positive attitude strengthens the immune system.

The power of thought

Perhaps you have read the old maxim which states: 'Thoughts produce acts, acts produce habits, and habits produce character.'

This belief is closely reflected by the wisdom of the Bible and emphasises the power of the mind to replicate what we think by acting out our thoughts. Proverbs 23:7 states: 'For as a man thinks in his heart, so is he.'

What are you thinking?

Whatever your thoughts are, you begin to speak them to yourself. Your words, whether negative or positive, have the power to influence your life. Self-talk is extremely powerful, because you believe what you hear yourself say.

One of the reasons for negative self-talk is the inability to get over the hurts of the past. When we hold on to the negatives of yesteryear and worry over our past, we cloud the present, nursing unhealed wounds, and blight our future with the apprehension and fear of more pain to come.

Many people live so much in the past that they cannot enjoy the present. Willie Jolley puts it this way: 'The past is supposed to be a place of reference, not a place of residence.'

**The past is past.
Get over it and move on.**

Accentuate the positive –

Just think: If you can begin to highlight the positive elements and eliminate the negatives in your life, you are at least halfway to a less stressful life!

Try improving your thinking style by asking God to renew your mind so that you can cope better with stressful situations.

Here are two very effective measures to help combat stress:

Promise box – This contains a number of encouraging passages of Scripture which you can use as positive affirmations. Place it in strategic points in your home or carry it in your handbag or briefcase.

Prayer partnership – This provides prayer cover for you, particularly in times when you are experiencing challenges and find it difficult to pray. The realisation that someone is standing in prayer with you is both comforting and strengthening.

In the book *Mind, Character and Personality* vol 2, p. 403, E. G. White states: 'A person whose mind is quiet and satisfied in God is in the pathway to health.'

HANDLING THE PRESSURE –
Achieving balance

If we took a critical look at our lives, most of us would find that at some point we have been out of balance in terms of the amount of time we give to our physical, emotional, spiritual and social well-being. We struggle sometimes to find the balance between work and leisure, sleep and wakefulness, rest and activity, solitude and sociability. It's at these times of struggle and imbalance that we encounter stress.

Our week consists of seven days. God gives us six days to work, and one to rest. This seven-day cycle of work and rest is a special blessing from God. It gives mankind an opportunity to press the pause button in his life, to 'Be still.' In this stillness we will have a better perspective of who we are, our purpose in life, and God's will for us. We are refreshed and rejuvenated to face the working week ahead of us.

Does your work and life activity bring more stress than satisfaction? Is it taking away from your time with God? Are you finding a good balance between your vocational, domestic and social aspirations?

Ecclesiastes has this summary about work-life balance:

'So what do we get from all our efforts and labour? In this life hard work is given to us by God. But this was not his original plan. In the beginning he made everything beautiful and created man in his own image. He put in man's heart a sense of destiny. . . . There is nothing better in life than for man to do good, which will bring him happiness as long as he lives. God wants man to enjoy his life and be happy, to find satisfaction in his work.' Ecclesiastes 3:9-13 *(The Clear Word)*.

Pause for reflection time with God

The fast pace of life often means that we are under threat of losing time for contemplating the eternal values which build up our spiritual life. The increasing competing priorities can push our time with God out of balance.

When we slow down the pace of life and stop our restless activity to be still with God, we are in a position to listen more effectively to him. Hearing God's voice is not so easy when we are rushing around preoccupied with so many other things.

Life brings with it so many disappointments. Learning how to rest in God gives us a quiet heart, a heart that is 'still' to hear from him and respond accordingly. We rest from our anxieties, our hurts, our restlessness when we rest in God. I have been greatly encouraged by a favourite text of mine found in Psalm 46:10: 'Be still and know that I am God.'

When we consider what the duty of man is, we put God in perspective by realising the purpose of our existence. Solomon reminds us how to prioritise our life:

'After all is said and done, there is only one thing that really matters: Reverence your heavenly Father and do what he says. That's the only thing that has meaning and lasts. So love God and keep his commandments. He loves you and has told you all you need to know. One day he will judge everything we have done in this life, including every secret thing, whether it was good or bad.' Ecclesiastes 12:13, 14 *(The Clear Word).*

When we acquire a true knowledge of God and his will for us, it makes us grounded in Christ, unmoved by the vicissitudes of life, and secure in the peace that he gives.

Today and every day dedicate some quiet time to spend with God alone, to meet with him, to see, to connect, to feel and to experience him. Then you will find peace.

PEACE – a recipe for tranquil moments of reflection

P – Pause. Stop and be still. Delight in the fact that you choose to 'be' rather than 'do' at this moment. Don't feel guilty about this time of seeming inactivity. Just enjoy it. Think of this as a time of renewal, when your energies are being replenished and you gain new strength to face the world again.

E – Environment. Retire to a treasured spot where you can easily unwind. Ensure that the lighting, the temperature and the furniture is comfortable and enhances a relaxing and reflective mood. Make this your personal area, a safe haven of retreat. You may wish to choose some appropriate music which adds to the ambience and aids your restful mode.

A – Attitude. Detox your mind. Getting rid of negative thoughts helps you to think more clearly and enhances general well-being. With a positive mindset you can face life with all its challenges, conquer the past with its disappointments and embrace the future with hope.

Encourage yourself and others. It lifts your mood and reminds you of what is possible.

C – Calm. The ability to bring body, mind and spirit into a state of rest. Try a soothing herbal tea like camomile, known for its calming properties, to relax the nerves and induce sleep.

Prayer is a powerful exercise which relieves the pressure and allows you to express hopes, hurts and joys. It enables you to connect with God, reflect and pace your thinking as you gain strength and wisdom to continue the journey of life.

E – Exercise. Engage in regular exercise; it's a great stress buster. Exercise improves the circulation, boosts immunity and maintains good health both mentally and physically. It also enhances rest.

A final word

I lay in a hospital bed, barely able to move and wondering what was happening to my health and my life in general. I had been forced to pause from the treadmill of life as my body was rebelling from the onslaught of excessive working hours and an overflowing agenda. This consisted of days full of ever-increasing activity and stress, late nights at the computer fulfilling more work demands and church commitments, and the inability to say 'No.'

It was then that I discovered how difficult it was to rest body, mind and spirit. Physically, I found it hard to relax as I was not used to sitting still for long periods of time. I was frustrated that I could not physically get around to undertake the numerous tasks waiting for me to complete. I was good at multitasking. Therefore, as I lay in hospital my mind was racing.

Since that time I have come a long way in realising the importance of being at rest and at peace with God, with myself and others. This has come from a realisation that I need to be doing less, or at least reframing my mindset about how much is humanly possible for me to accomplish without compromising my well-being. The biggest lesson however, is realising that I am not in control, God is and I can safely hand over the reins of my life to him.

The gospels record the advice Jesus gave to his disciples when they returned from their preaching tour. The twelve were encouraged by Jesus to come away from the pressures of the day for some quality time of rest, relaxation and renewal.

Mark 6:31 states: 'And he said to them, "Come aside by yourselves to a deserted place and rest a while." ' *(New King James Version.)*